Carving Fancy Walking Sticks

Tom Wolfe

4880 Lower Valley Road, Atglen, PA 19310 USA

Contents

Copyright © 2002 by Tom Wolfe
Library of Congress Card Number: 2001098943

Designed by John P. Cheek
Cover design by Bruce M. Waters
Type set in Korinna BT

ISBN: 0-7643-1565-X
Printed in China

Published by Schiffer Publishing Ltd.
4880 Lower Valley Road
Atglen, PA 19310
Phone: (610) 593-1777; Fax: (610) 593-2002
E-mail: Schifferbk@aol.com
Please visit our web site catalog at
www.schifferbooks.com
We are always looking for people to write books on
new and related subjects. If you have an idea for a
book please contact us at the above address.

This book may be purchased from the publisher.
Include $3.95 for shipping.
Please try your bookstore first.
You may write for a free catalog.

In Europe, Schiffer books are distributed by
Bushwood Books
6 Marksbury Ave.
Kew Gardens
Surrey TW9 4JF England
Phone: 44 (0) 20 8392-8585;
Fax: 44 (0) 20 8392-9876
E-mail: Bushwd@aol.com
Free postage in the U.K., Europe; air mail at cost.

Introduction

Any old stick will do as a walking stick, as long as it is strong enough to hold the walker's weight as they use to pole vault across a stream or push themselves up a steep path. Trimmed to the proper length and heft, the stick becomes a valuable part of the hiker's gear, and they would never think of leaving home or camp without it.

It is little wonder then that over many months or years of use, the stick often takes on a personality. Its curves and knots become as familiar as the wrinkles on the hiker's face. This has led more than a few outdoors people to give their walking sticks names. Sometimes when I'm in the woods I will hear a voice. I turn around, thinking someone's talking to me, only to find him or her deep in conversation with a piece of wood.

Maybe that's why there is so much interest in wood spirits in general and fancy walking sticks and canes in particular. In a small way carving a face or an animal into the wood gives a face to the personality that resides there. Of the pieces I carve and sell, the walking sticks and canes are among the most popular. And when we carve them in class, there is a noticeable excitement among the students.

I hope that you will feel this, too, as you carve your walking stick. This book is meant to take you step by step through the process of creating a new walking stick. The head I carve is a free design, done without a pattern like I carve wood spirits. For those who are more comfortable with carving from patterns, there are

several to choose from in the back of the book. In either case the steps to the carving are the same. Some of you may wish to simply add a face to your old walking stick. Using the carving techniques here should let you do that just as easily.

I hope you enjoy the carving and will gets hours of fun and exploration with your new walking stick.

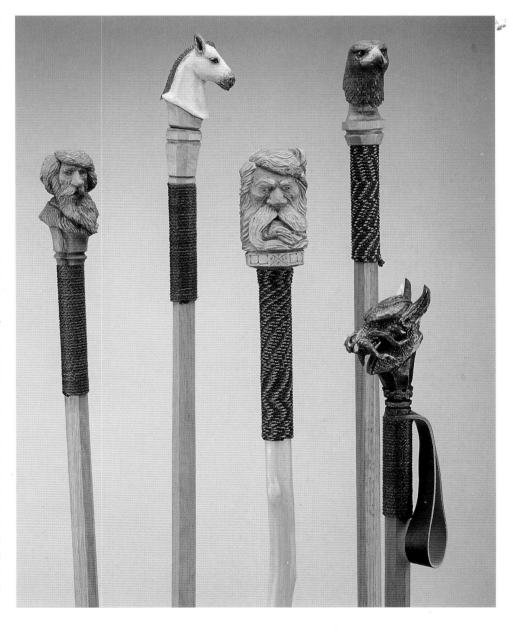

Getting Started

The shaft of the walking stick is just a poplar sapling I found. I skinned the bark off of it to give it a clean look, but you can leave the bark on if it pleases you. A good hiking stick should be no taller than the top of your head and no shorter than your chin. The idea is that it can help you move down hills or across streams, or to lean on for a rest!

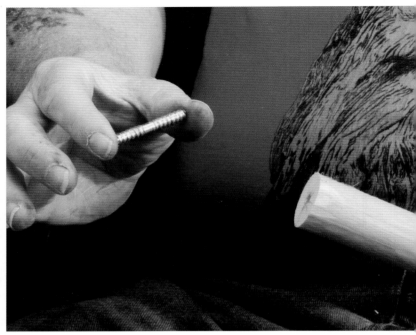

One end of the stick should be cut of for a flat surface. This is where we will attach the carved head. A double-ended screw will go into the center of this end.

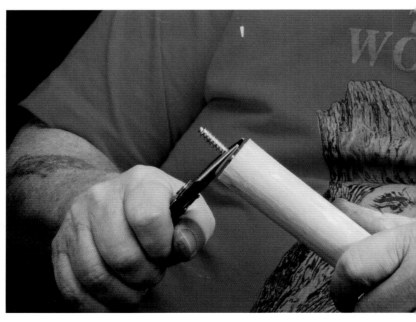

Drill a pilot hole into the shaft, then insert the screw using pliers.

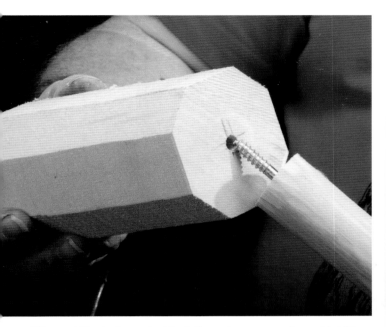

Whoops! The hole on the block I'm going to carve is too big! I'll show you how to fix that.

Now the screw fits tightly. I will glue it well when I'm done carving so the joint is a little stronger.

Slide a thin wood chip into the hole; that should take up some of the extra space.

The block should fit snugly against the stick.

The Carving

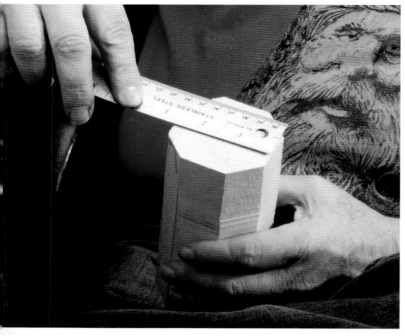

This is a two-and-a-half inch block of basswood, with the corners knocked off to make it octagonal. You could start with any size and shape you want.

Mark a place on the block and the stick so that you can realign them accurately every time you put them back together.

I'm marking about an inch-and-a-half from the bottom to leave room for a good base on the carving. I use a pen so it's easier to see in the pictures, but I recommend you use a pencil.

Trace the outline of the stick on the block so you have a reference point while carving.

Make a cut with a large V-tool along the line drawn for the base. Do it with a scooping motion toward yourself, using your wrist instead of pulling or pushing.

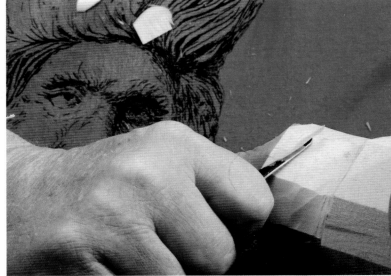

Progress. Make sure you retain the octagon shape for now.

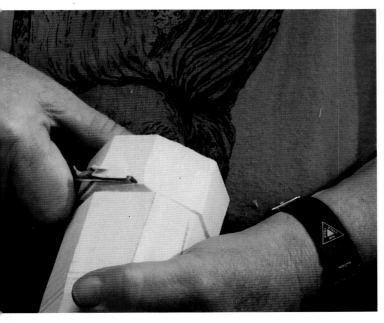

Narrow the base by carving down from the V-cut, going all around. I don't feel it's necessary to use a pattern for this carving; if you learn to make a face without a pattern, you'll always know how to make the face. Just start with a nose and let it flow from there.

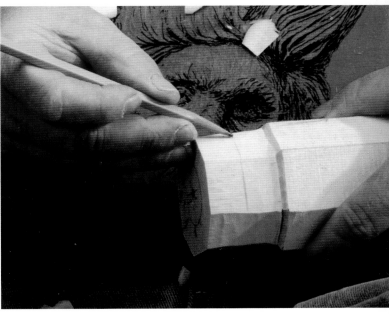

About halfway down the base, make another mark all the way around.

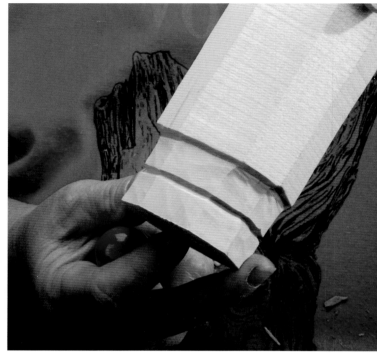

The finished V-cut.

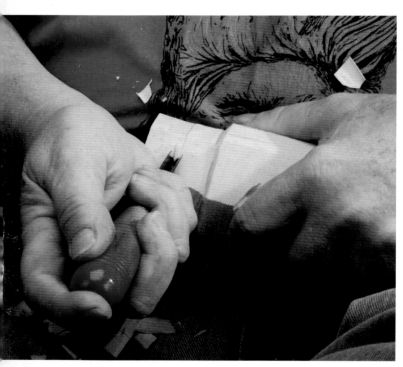

With a V-tool, make a cut similar to the first one.

I'll also make a new V-cut where the first one was carved away.

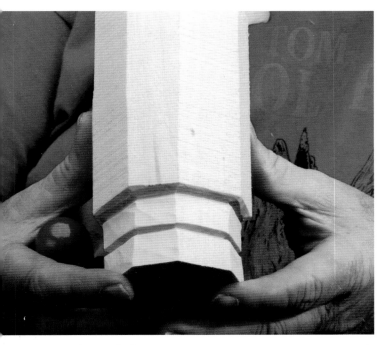

This reinforces the line.

Now I'm cutting down from the bottom V-cut to taper the base even more, but still keeping that octagon shape.

Progress. I've carved down almost to the shape of the staff.

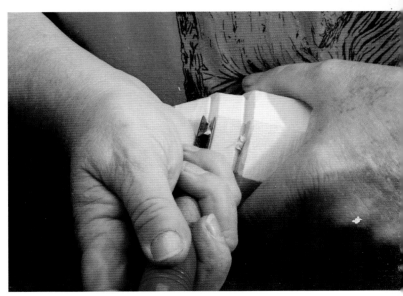

Go back in with the V-tool to reinforce the line.

9

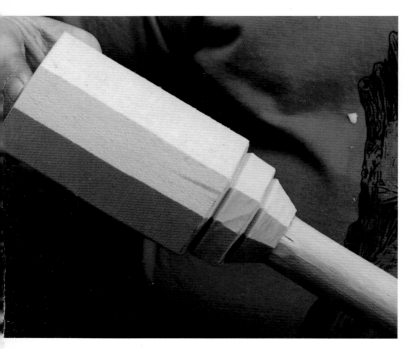

Place the carving back on the staff from time to time to make sure everything still lines up.

Carving the face begins with marking the bridge of the nose.

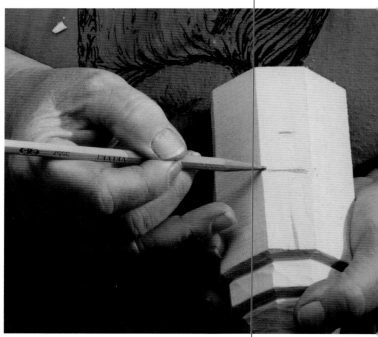

Then mark the bottom of the nose,

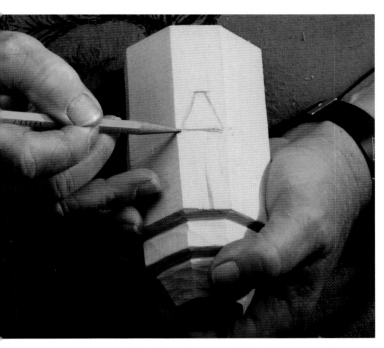

Finally make a triangle where the nose will be. The nose is the dominant part of the caricature, and the carving should start with it.

Cut a wedge out of the bridge of the nose with two cuts of the knife, one down at the brow and the second up at the top of the nose.

Before the carving begins, I spray the wood generously with a half-and-half mixture of water and rubbing alcohol. The water makes the wood carve more smoothly and the alcohol helps it dry up. Some people will even soak the block overnight. Just make sure you make all your marks in pencil, because ink will bleed.

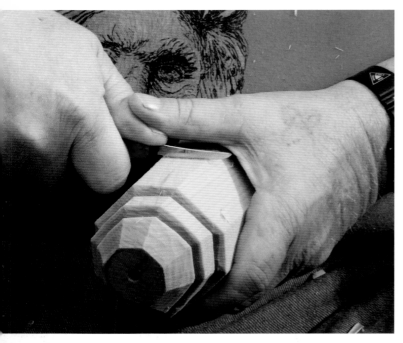

Make a stop cut at the bottom of the nose by rocking the knife back and forth. The nose can be as big or small as you want it, but remember it will gauge the size of the face.

The profile, so far.

Cut back to stop cut along the surface of the upper lip under the nose. This should be an angled cut and should go as deeply as you want

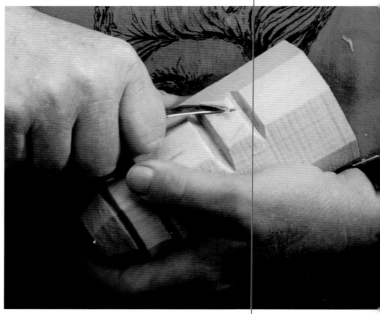

Nip out the sides of the nose, starting at the line and moving out toward the cheek. You can use either a knife or a gouge.

A good knife will flex and follow the curvature of what you're carving.

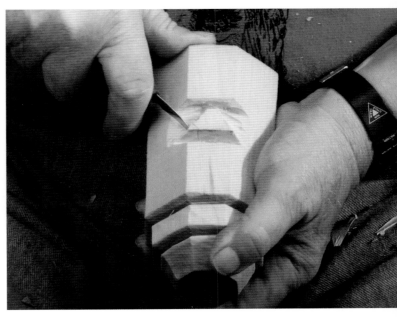

Cut the notch for the nostrils by making a stop cut across the corner of the nose...

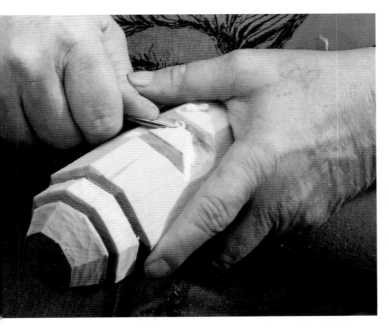

Use a gouge to smooth out any overcuts you've made with the knife.

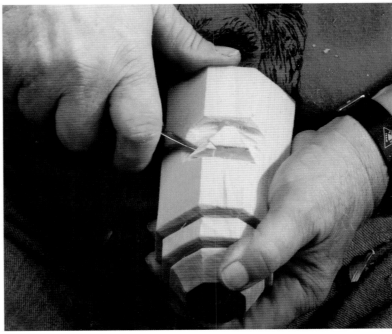

and, then, cutting back to it from the cheek. The piece should pop right off.

Progress.

Progress. See how smooth the cuts are with the alcohol solution? You can spray again when you cut down to a dry spot.

I'm taking some wood off of the top edge, but I'm leaving a lump on the side of the head for what will be a feather, or leaves, or some kind of ornament.

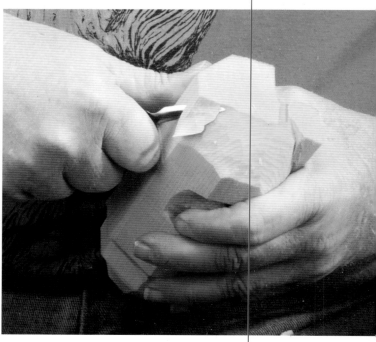

Continue rounding the head.

Progress.

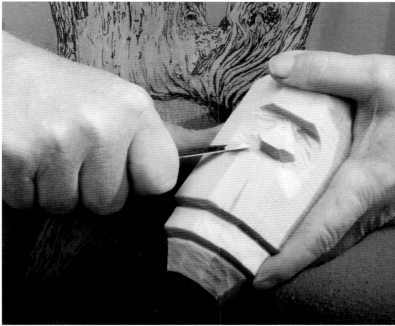

Returning to the face, remove some more wood out to get rid of some of the fullness around the mouth.

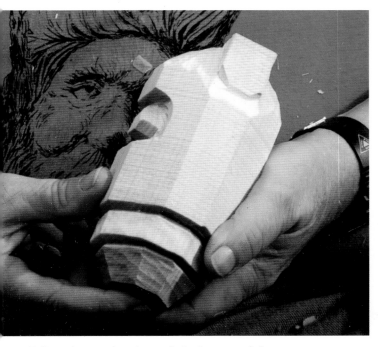

Relieve the wood underneath the lump you left.

The smile lines are carved by, first, making a stop cut at the side of the nose, beside the nostril.

Along the cheek make a second cut at a 45-degree angle to the first, with the knife at a 45-degree angle down.

Progress.

The third cut comes up along the surface of the lip at a 45-degree angle. A triangular piece should pop right out defining the smile line. Do this on both sides of the nose.

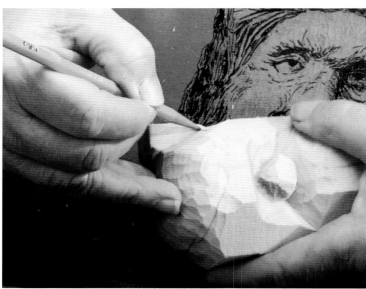

Mark a hairline.

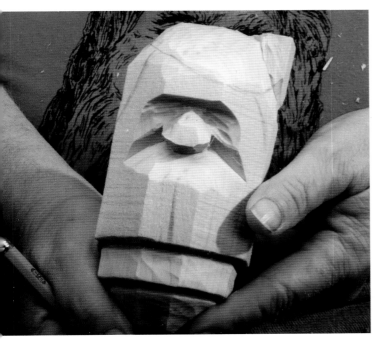

Progress.

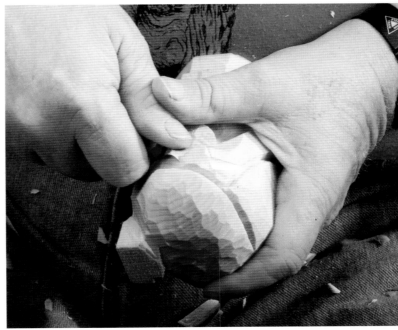

Cut up to the stop from the face, using a knife.

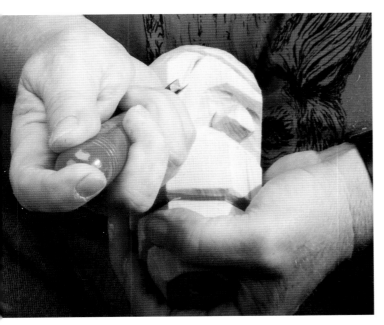

Follow the hairline with a V-tool to create a stop cut.

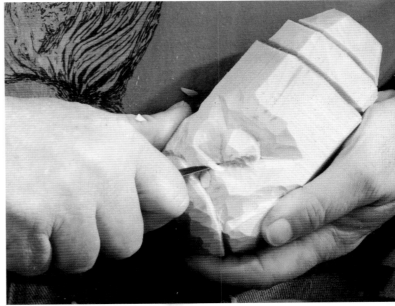

While I'm here, I'll soften the eyebrow a little bit so he's not frowning so much.

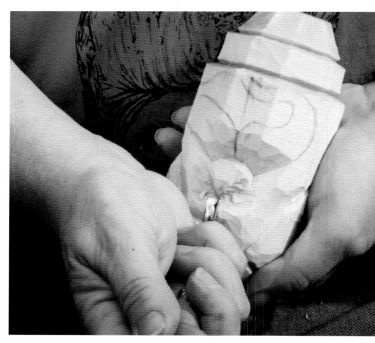
Separate the eyebrows with a gouge.

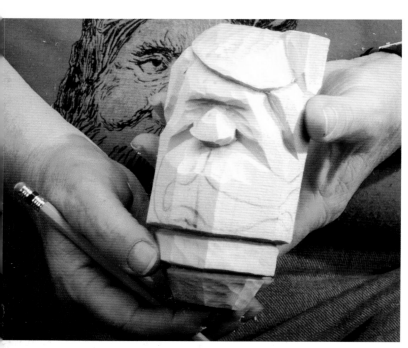
Progress. This is a good time to mark the beard and the moustache. I'd like them to flow around to one side of the head in sort of a windswept look.

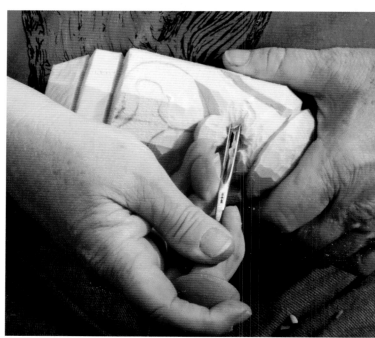
While you're in there with the gouge, you can also widen the socket for the eye.

Progress.

Progress.

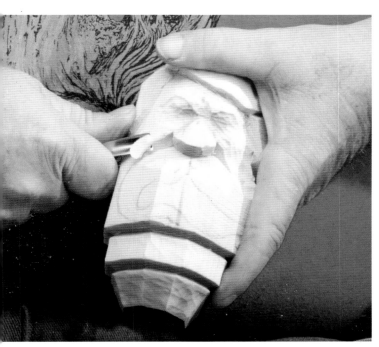

Carve under the cheekbones with a flat gouge. This will give them a strong definition.

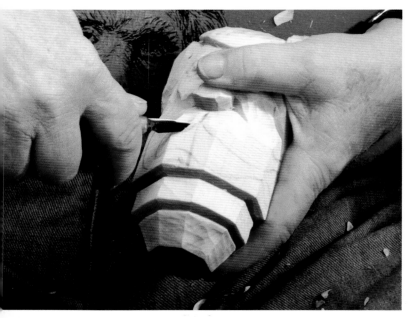

Define the mouth area using three cuts. First cut straight in on the underside of the moustache.

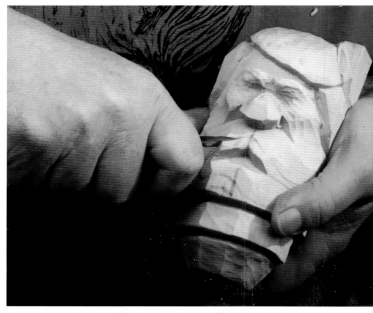

There's still too much moustache in there, so I'm cutting away some more wood from it using the same process. Cut a stop along the new moustache lines.

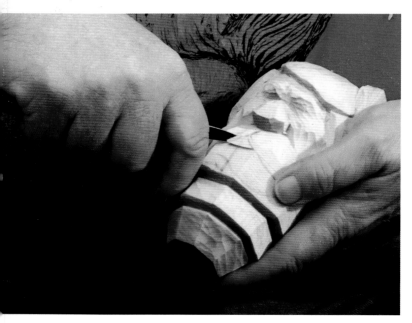

Next come up from the mouth, making the third side of the triangle and popping out the center piece.

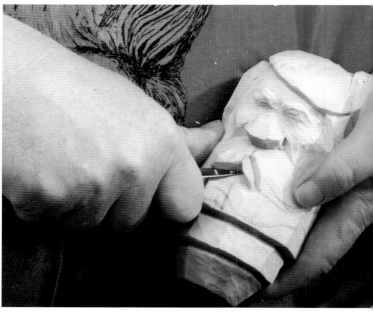

and popping out the excess from below.

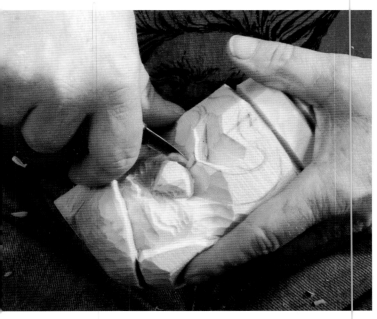

Three more cuts define the two sides of the moustache. Cut at an angle toward the center from one side…

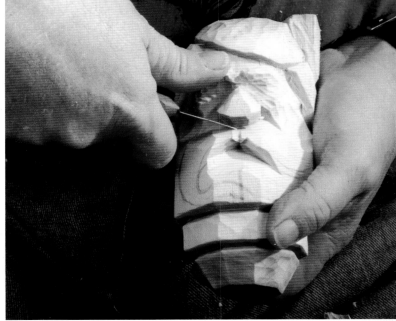

Then under the nose clip off the top of the V-cut you have formed.

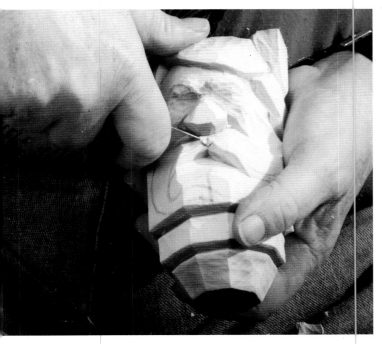

Another three cuts will establish the indentation under the nose.

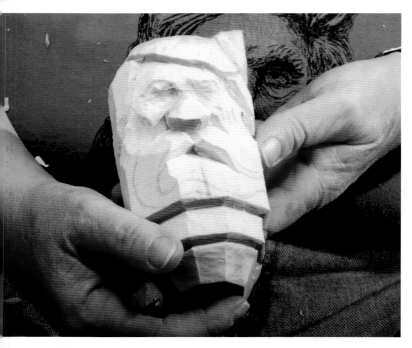

Progress.

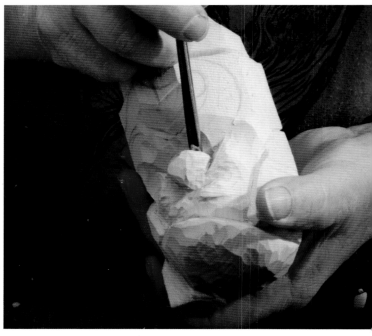

Make nostrils by pushing a half round straight up the nose! There's no need to use any kind of prying motion, since that could break the nose off.

Since the face is now a little better defined, I can work a little more on the nose. I'm just rounding it off a little.

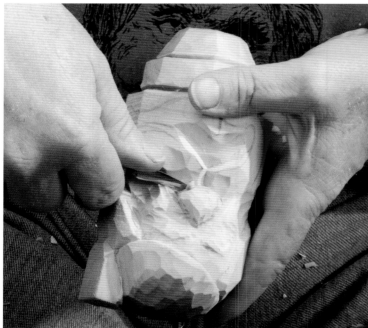

Use the tip of the knife to carefully clip off the cut you just made with the half round.

Progress.

Progress on the nose.

To make the flange of the nostrils, start at the tip of the nose with the half round and move up and over the nostril. When you get around to the up and down direction of the grain, the piece will pop right off.

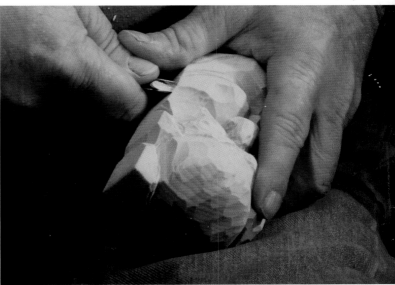

Using a large V-tool, follow the lines you drew for the beard and moustache. Make the lines as sweeping and flowing as possible. Avoid short jerky motions, and do not let two lines cross to form an "X."

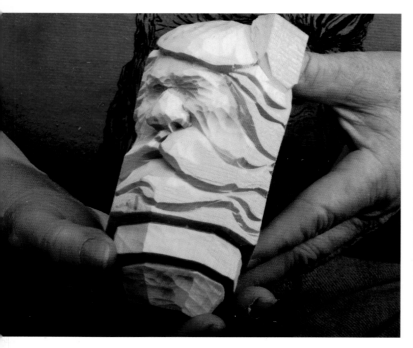

Progress.

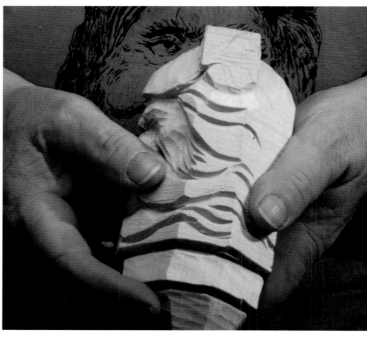

Remember the lump of wood I left on his head? I think I'll carve leaves out of it. I'll mark it first. The hairline will fade into a stem. Draw the major lines in pencil...

The lines of the hair run around the back of the head also.

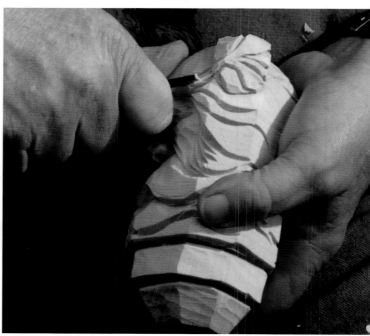

and follow them with the V-tool.

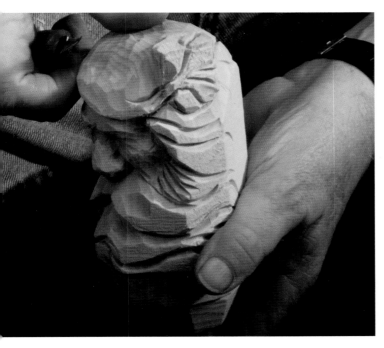

Progress.

Progress.

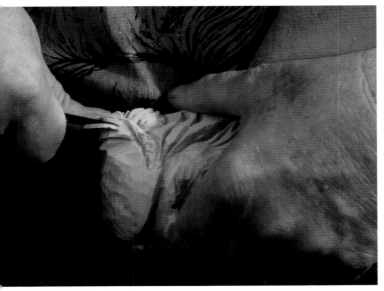

Using a small veiner, I'm adding some knots for the bark of the twig. This detail helps establish what is hair and what is not! I also use the veiner to add smaller veins to the leaves. Use the knife to round off the sharp edges as the leaves start to take shape.

Now I will add detail to the area around the mouth. I would like to work in some leaves and twigs in this area, too. Draw the major lines…

and use the V-tool to carve them.

Progress.

Use the veiner to create hair texture.

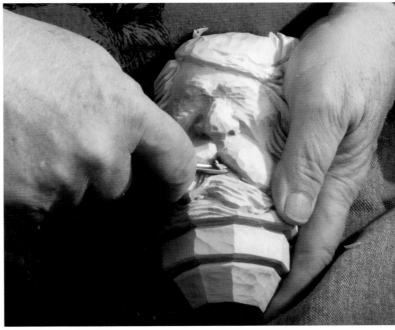

One small gouge mark will define the lower lip.

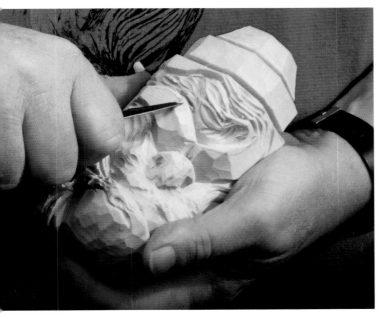

I'm using the knife to soften the moustache.

Clean the corners out with the knife.

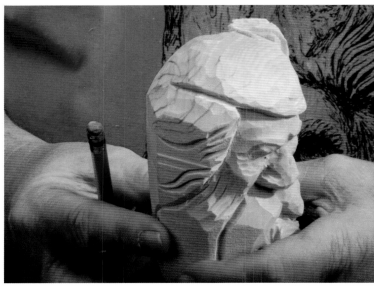

Now I will carve the hair—there's lots to carve! I've already carved in a part, so that will help determine how the hair will fall on the head and around the face. Again draw the major lines.

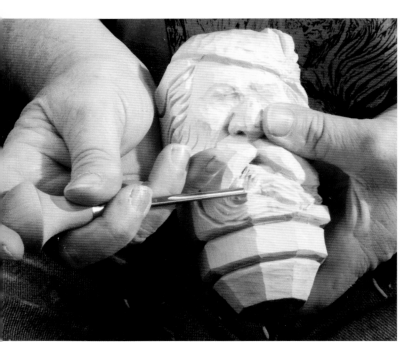

Using the small gouge, add texture to the stems of the twigs, setting them apart from the hair.

Use the veiner and the V-tool to carve in the hair texture. Use the V-tool to make the major cuts first, and then use the veiner for the finer details.

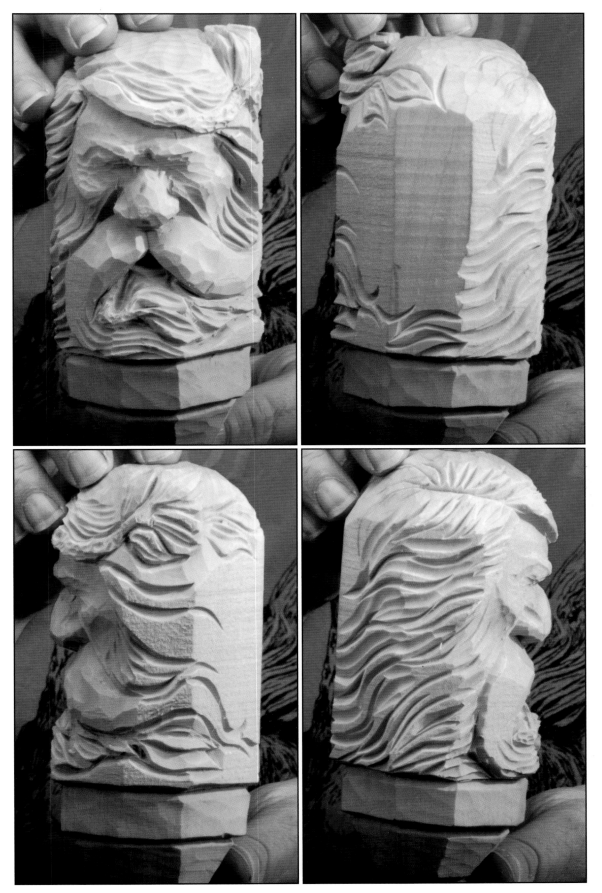

Progress.

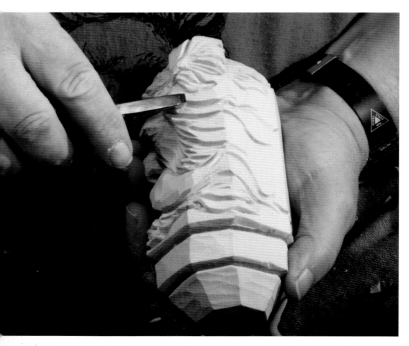

I think I'll add another leaf here, starting with these lines I've carved with the V-tool.

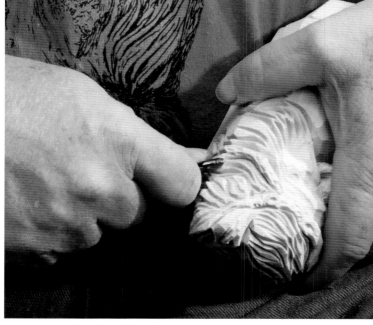

I'm defining the stems using a 24-degree V-tool, which will create deeper shadows. Two cuts with the knife will give you the same effect.

The leaf is starting to take shape.

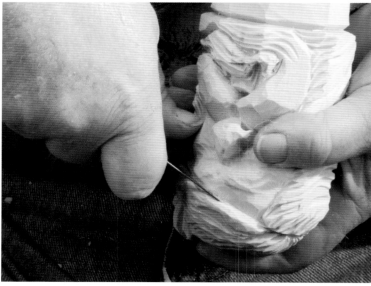

I also want to deepen the hairline at the top of the forehead. First make a stop cut along the hairline,

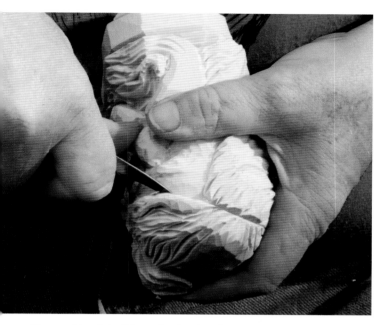

Then cut back to it from the forehead.

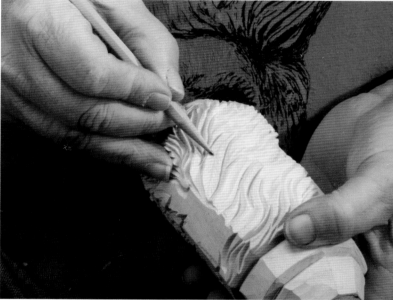

Continue to carve the hair, looking for places to add interesting details. This looks like a good place to add a feather.

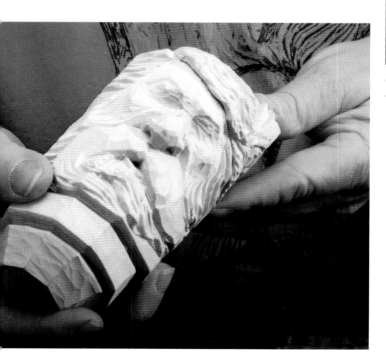

Progress.

The rough carving of the hair establishes the character of the head.

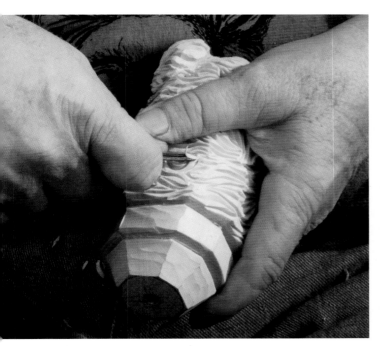

Now I will go back in with the veiner and add the finer texture. These softer lines show up really well when you paint the piece.

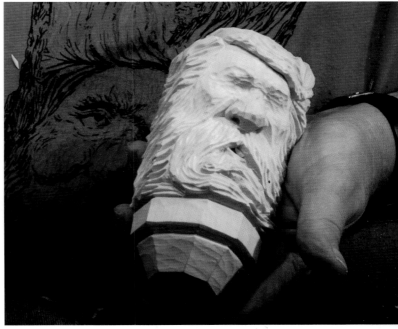

Progress.

You can also use the veiner for the hair texture on the moustache.

Smooth the eye sockets out to make room for the eye.

I also will narrow the nose down a little, with a gouge.

I will show you a couple of different ways to do the eyes. I usually use one of my eye punches (available from Woodcraft). Let's say that this is an eye socket.

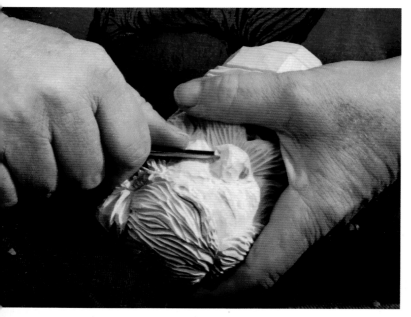

The flare of the nostril will need to be redefined, too, by going over it with the gouge.

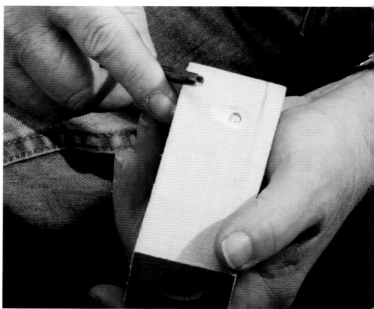

Press the punch straight into the wood, rocking it gently to form the curve of the eyeball.

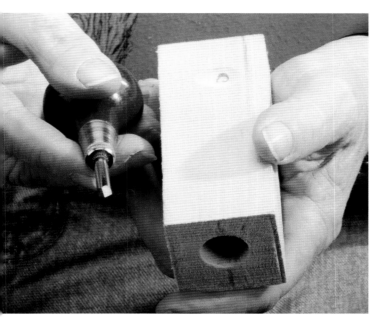

Here is a tool I've ground flat on the bottom and beveled at 45 degrees. It's great for detail work.

The result.

It's great to use in the corners of eyes.

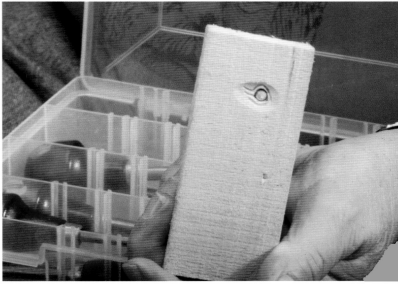

With the curve of the eyeball and the corners set with the punches, carefully carve eyelids above and below the eye.

This eyepunch has been half ground off. I'll use it to make the iris.

Another way is to start with the half-ground eye punch. It gives more of a sleepy-eyed look.

Apply it at the top of the eyeball for this result. These punches are great because they keep paint from spreading into unwanted places on your carving.

Use the knife to nip out the corners of the eye.

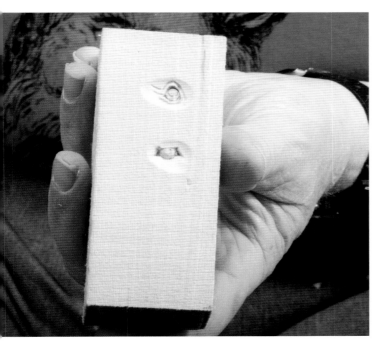

The result

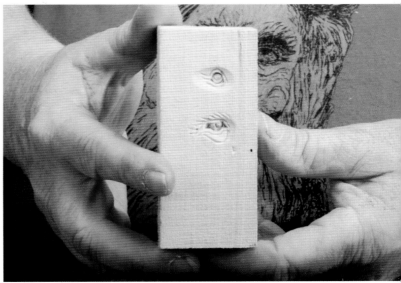

A smaller half-ground eye punch will make the iris. I also carved some eyelashes and an extra bag under the eye.

Use the V-tool to make the eyelids. It's best to start at the top and work down once in each direction, instead of trying to do it all in one motion.

For our carving, mark a dot on each side of the nose where the tear duct belongs. Make sure they are an even distance from the center.

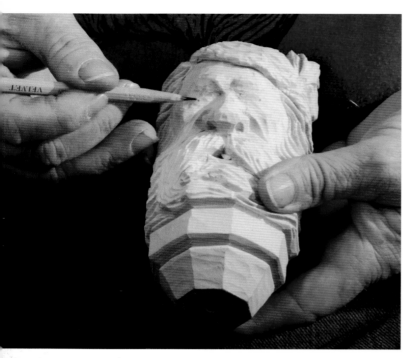

Put a dot where the outside corners of the eyes belong.

Repeat on the other side for this result.

To begin carving the eye, make a triangle shape, using three small cuts to form the tear duct.

Do a similar three-cut notch to form the outer corners of the eyes.

Use the V-tool to connect the two triangles above and below the eye.

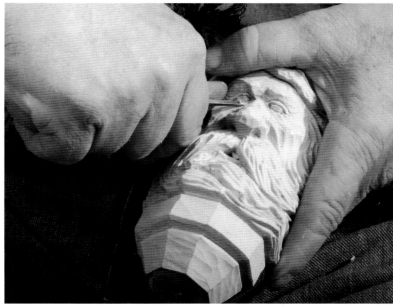

Use the V-tool or veiner to carve the eyelids above and below.

Progress.

Finally add a couple wrinkles and smile lines to show age. I've used an eye punch to make the iris. You can make the eyes looking anywhere you want.

I almost forgot the feather. I'll make a notch with two cuts of the knife to make it look more realistic.

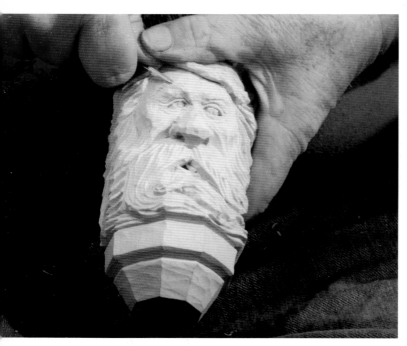

Now we can add the eyebrows. The veiner is great for this.

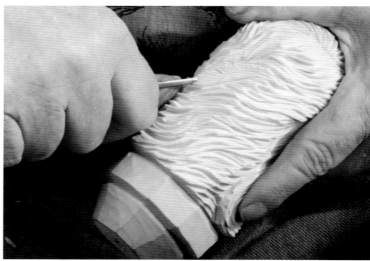

Use the veiner to make the vanes in the feather.

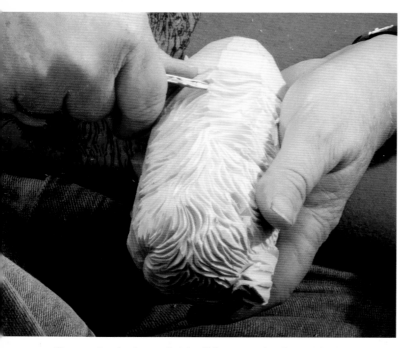

The carving is almost finished! I'm going back over the hair with the veiner to soften it up a bit.

The finished feather.

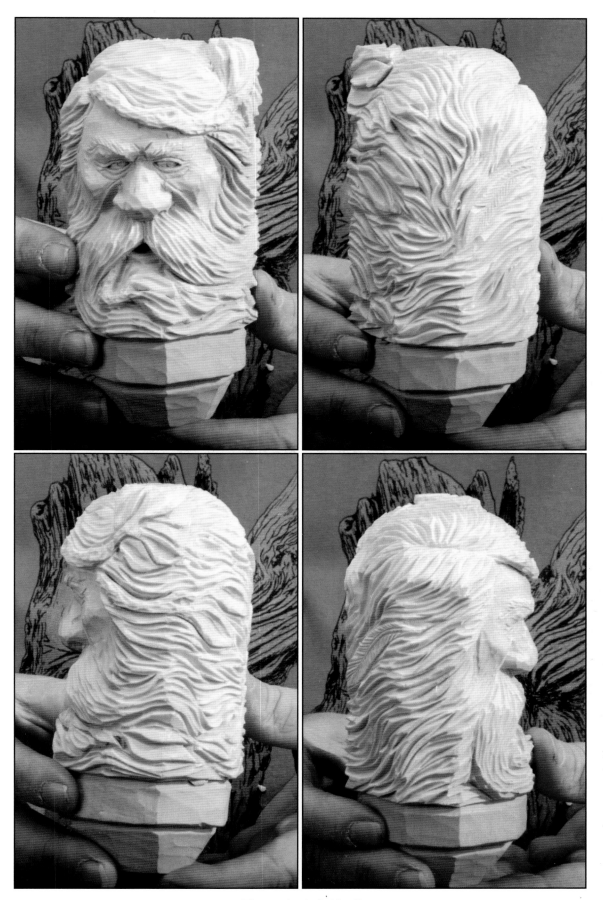

The carving is finished!

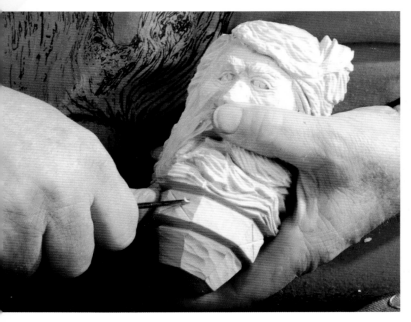

To dress up the base a little I begin with a veiner and carve a cross on every other segment

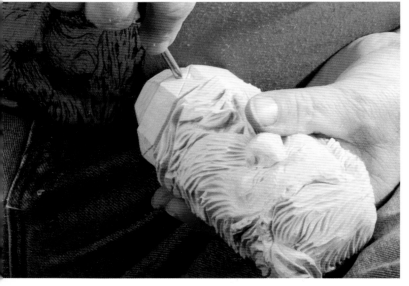

Using the L-shaped punch, add more designs on the base by going between the lines of the cross.

On the alternating sides you can add a pattern just using the punch.

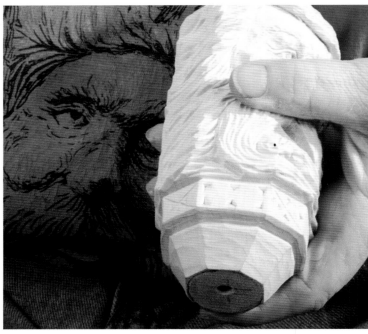

Progress.

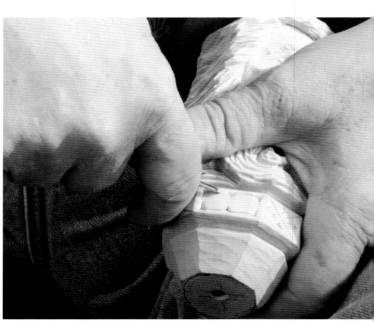

Connect the punch marks in the corners and middle using veiner.

42

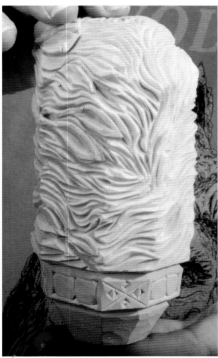

The finished carving ready for painting.

Painting

Blend a little red into the nose and cheeks to give them a blush.

The paints I use are artist's oils, thinned with turpentine into a stain. I start with a flesh color I mixed using a little raw sienna, a dab of flesh color, and mostly white. For a darker complexion I add some burnt sienna. Cover all the flesh areas of the face.

I'll give the hair and beard an undercoat of yellow to start, and then go back and tone it down with some sienna.

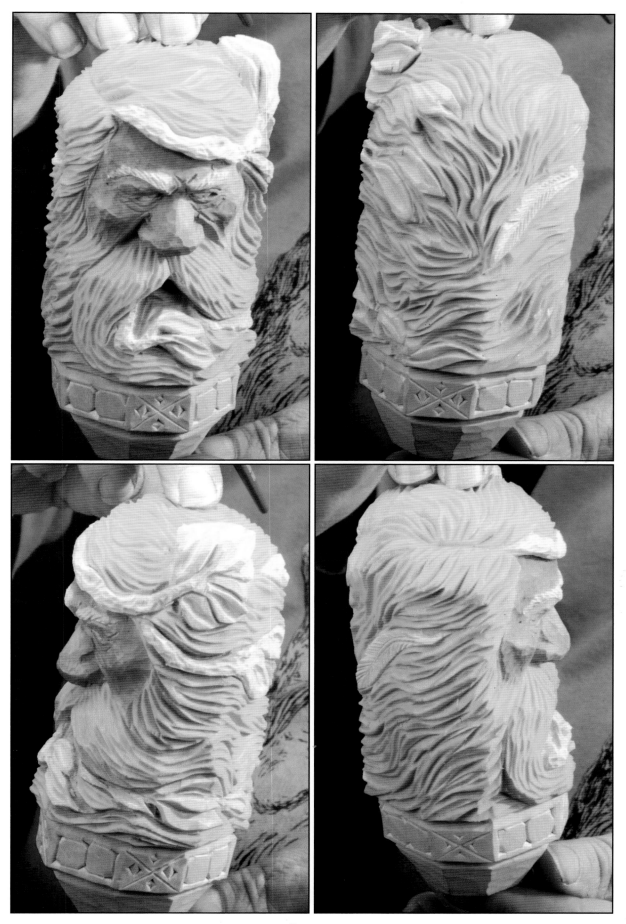

Progress.

Progress.

Apply burnt sienna to the stems and twigs.

The leaves, of course, are painted green.

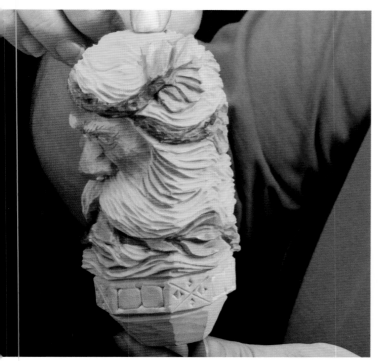

Progress.

Add some flecks of white for a more realistic look.

I'll make that feather a bluebird feather, and give it a white quill.

The eyes will also be blue. First paint the whole iris with a darker shade of blue, and then paint a lighter shade of blue in the middle that goes almost out to the edge.

You can use a black marker to dot in the pupils.

Add the whites of the eyes.

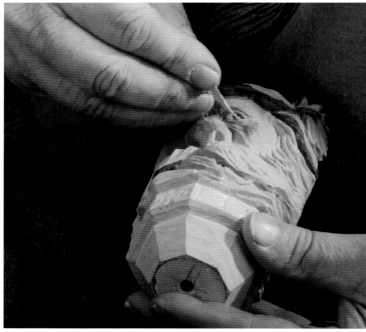

A tiny dot of white is all you need for the catchlight in the eye. Wherever you decide to put it, make sure the other side matches it exactly. A light coat of Deft semi-gloss spray will seal the carving with a nice finish. Make sure you let it dry thoroughly.

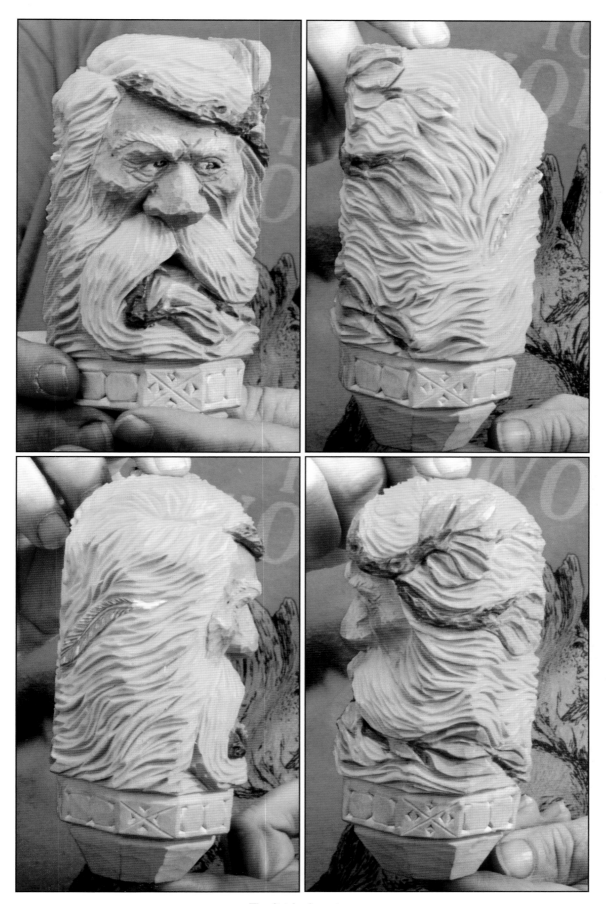

The finished carving.

Now I'm going to antique the carving. The solution I use is made of mostly turpentine, some linseed oil, and a tiny bit of burnt sienna. Brush on a generous coat.

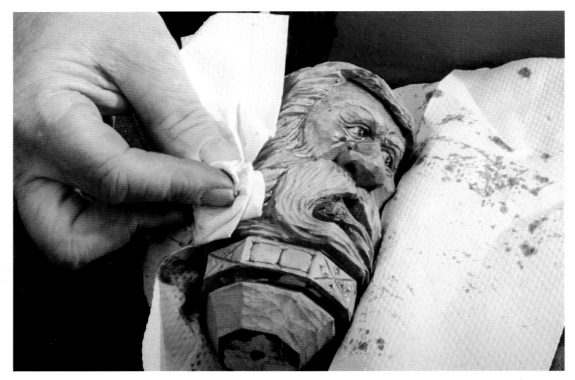

The idea is to cover it with the solution until every surface is covered and then to blot off as much as possible. Be careful you don't wipe it, because that could mess up the painting you just finished.

The antiqued carving.

Final Steps

Place the head on the shaft and let it dry at least an hour; to let it fully bond, it should sit overnight.

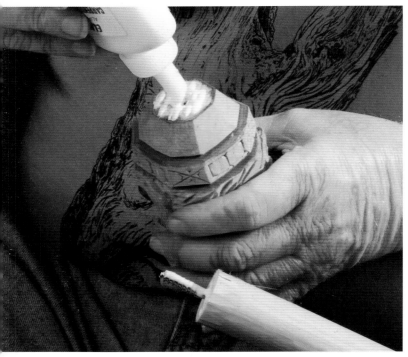

We are ready to put the carving on the staff. Regular wood or white glue works well. Put glue on the carving, the staff, the screw, and into the screw hole.

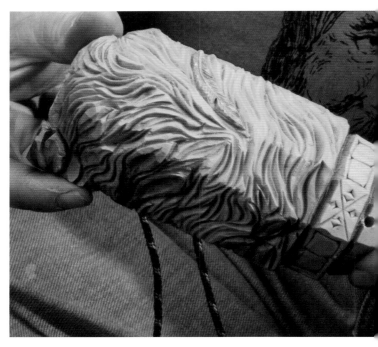

To finish the piece nicely, I'm going to wrap it with cord. First, I drill a hole at the base of the carving. Make sure the glue is dry before you do this. Also make sure that the drill bit is the same thickness as the cord you are planning to use.

You'll need piece of nylon string (available at any hardware store) 12 to 15 feet long. Using a match or candle, hold one end in the flame until the fibers begin to melt, then jam it in the hole you drilled. Let it cool and dry, and then you can begin wrapping it. You may find, as I did that the It looks like I made a mistake; I can't wrap the cord to fit on that tapered base very securely.

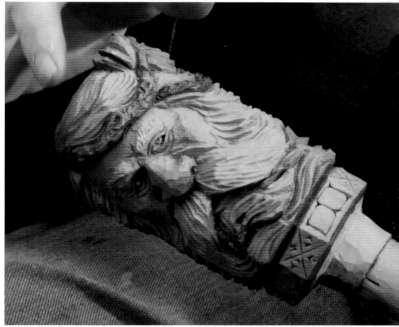

Progress.

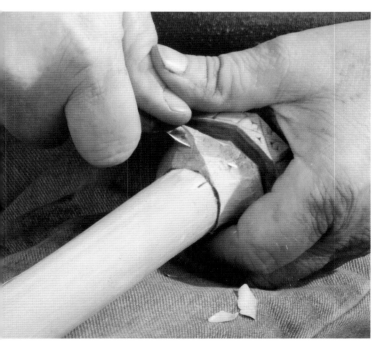

To fix the mistake, I first have to cut back the lower base so there is far less of a bevel.

Burn the string again, put it back in the drilled hole, and begin wrapping. If you wrap tightly and consistently, the colors on the string will make a nice pattern.

When you've wrapped as much string as you like on the piece, drill a hole in the staff, going all the way through.

Progress.

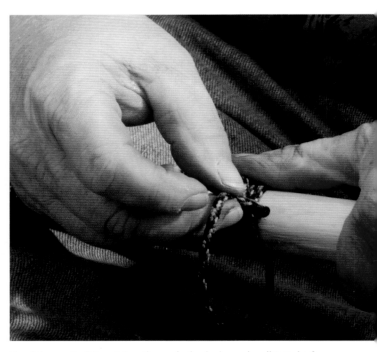

Feed the end of the string through the hole and pull it tight from the other side.

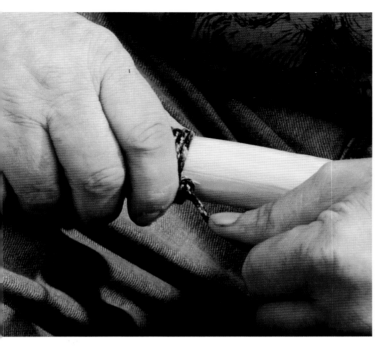

Tie a knot.

Burn the end around the knot to melt it together.

Cut off the loose end, close to the knot, but not too close.
Sometimes I'll leave the loose end and string beads on it.

Now I am antiquing the area I had to cut away. You could antique
the wrap, too, if you wanted.

The finished project. The only thing left is a light coat of Deft spray over the entire staff.

Gallery

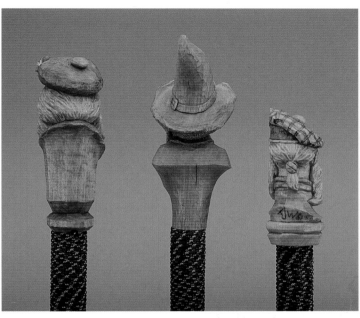

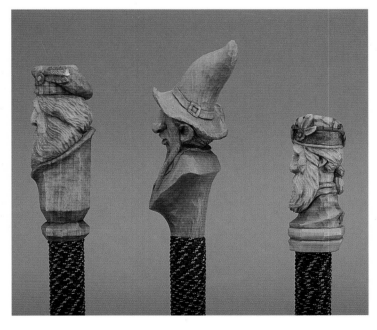